Play Piano with...
Lady GaGa, Adele,
Alicia Keys etc...

Published by

Wise Publications
14-15 Berners Street, London W1T 3LJ, UK

Exclusive Distributors:

Music Sales Limited
Distribution Centre, Newmarket Road,
Bury St Edmunds, Suffolk IP33 3YB, UK

Music Sales Pty Limited
20 Resolution Drive,
Caringbah, NSW 2229, Australia

Order No. AM1002749
ISBN 978-1-84938-963-1
This book © Copyright 2011 Wise Publications,
a division of Music Sales Limited.

Printed in the EU

Edited by Jenni Wheeler
Backing tracks by Paul Honey and Chris Hussey.

CD mixed and mastered by Jonas Persson.

Your Guarantee of Quality
As publishers, we strive to produce every book
to the highest commercial standards.
The music has been freshly engraved and the book has
been carefully designed to minimise awkward page turns
and to make playing from it a real pleasure.
Particular care has been given to specifying acid-free,
neutral-sized paper made from pulps which have not been
elemental chlorine bleached. This pulp is from farmed
sustainable forests and was produced with special regard
for the environment.
Throughout, the printing and binding have been planned
to ensure a sturdy, attractive publication which should
give years of enjoyment.
If your copy fails to meet our high standards,
please inform us and we will gladly replace it.

www.musicsales.com

Play Piano with...
Lady GaGa, Adele, Alicia Keys etc...

WISE PUBLICATIONS
PART OF THE MUSIC SALES GROUP

LONDON / NEW YORK / PARIS / SYDNEY / COPENHAGEN / BERLIN / MADRID / HONG KONG / TOKYO

Cry Me Out

Words & Music by Pixie Lott, Mads Hauge,
Phil Thornalley & Colin Campsie

1. I got your e-mails. You just don't get fe-males, now, do___ you?___
2. When I found out how you messed me a-bout I was bro - ken.___ Back

cry me out. You'll have to cry me out._____ The

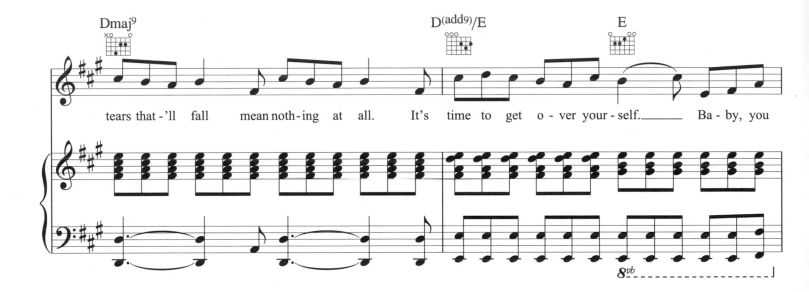

tears that -'ll fall mean noth-ing at all. It's time to get o-ver your-self._____ Ba - by, you

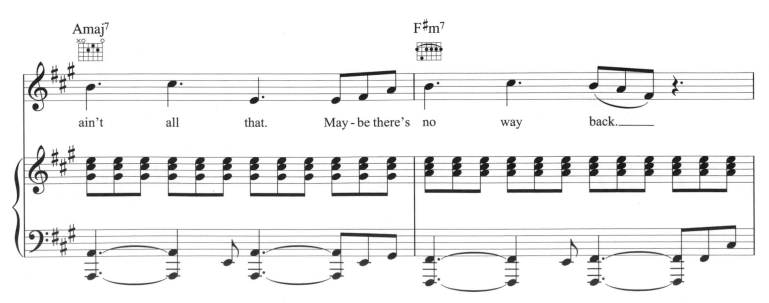

ain't all that. May-be there's no way back._____

You can keep talk-ing but, ba - by, I'm walk-ing a - way.____

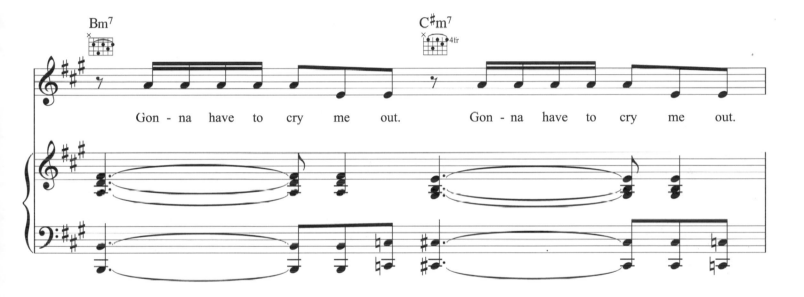

Gon - na have to cry me out. Gon - na have to cry me out.

Boy, there ain't no doubt: gon-na have to cry me out. Won't hurt a lit-tle bit, boy, bet-ter get used to it.

You can keep talk-ing but, ba - by, I'm walk-ing a - way.

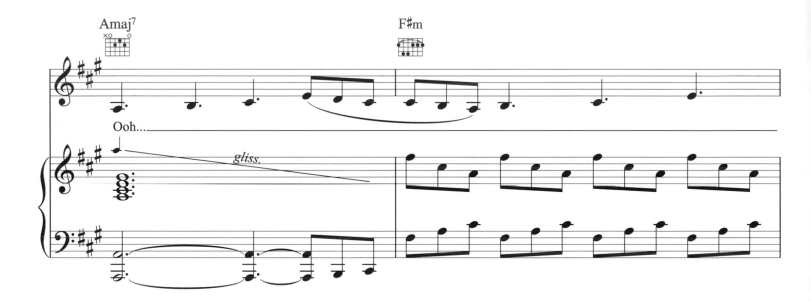

Ooh...

Ooh...

You'll have to

cry me out. You'll have to cry me out._____ The

tears that -'ll fall mean noth-ing at all. It's time to get o - ver your-self._____ Ba - by, you

ain't all that. May - be there's no way back._____

You can keep talk-ing but, ba - by, I'm walk-ing a - way._____ You'll have to

Empire State Of Mind
(Part II) Broken Down

Words & Music by Alicia Keys, Sylvia Robinson, Shawn Carter, Angela Hunte,
Bert Keyes, Alexander Shuckburgh & Janet Sewell

Noise is al - ways loud; there are si - rens all_ a - round,_ and the streets are mean._
Such a melt - ing pot;_ on the cor - ner sell - ing rock;_ preach - ers pray to God._

If I can make_ it here,_ I can make it an - y - where;_ that's what_ they say._
Hail a gyp - sy cab;_ takes me down from Har - lem to_ the Brook - lyn Bridge._

Bmaj7   C#

F#

See-ing my face in lights, or my name in mar-quees found down on Broad-way.
Some-one sleeps at night with a hun-ger for more than an emp-ty fridge.

Bmaj7   C#

A#

E-ven if it ain't all it seems, I got a pock-et-ful of dreams; ba-by, I'm from New
I'm-a make it by an-y means; I got a pock-et-ful of dreams, ba-by, I'm from

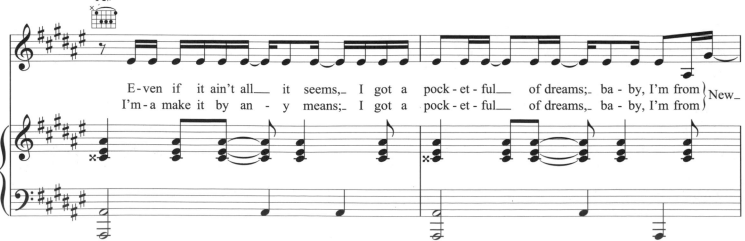

14

York. ___ Con-crete jun-gle where dreams are made___ of; there's noth-ing you can't___ do,___ now you're in New___ York.___ These streets will make you feel brand___ new, big lights will in - spire___ you;___ hear it for New___ York, New___ York, New___ York!___ ___ York!___

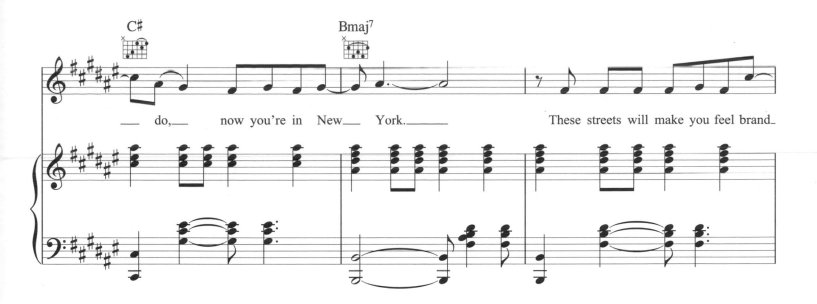

do,___ now you're in New___ York._____ These streets will make you feel brand

___ new, big lights will in - spire_____ you;___ hear it for New___

___ York!_____

Halo

Words & Music by Ryan Tedder, Beyoncé Knowles
& Evan Bogart

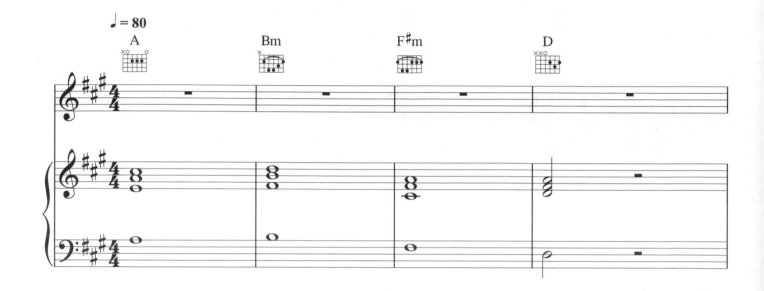

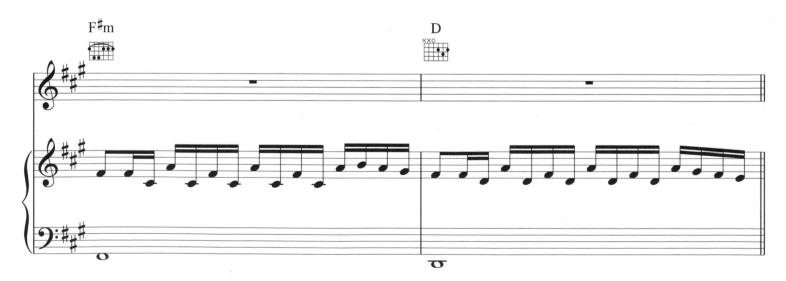

a - gain.} It's like I've been a - wak - ened,_____ ev -'ry rule I had you break - ing.____

It's the risk that I'm tak - ing._____ I ain't nev - er gon - na shut you out.____

Ev -'ry-where I'm look - ing now____ I'm sur-round-ed by your_ em - brace.

Ba - by, I can see your ha - lo._____ You know you're my sav - ing grace.___

23

Make You Feel My Love

Words & Music by Bob Dylan

1. When the rain is blow-ing in your face, and the whole world is on
2. When the eve-ning shad-ows and the stars ap-pear, and there is no one there to dry

your case,___
your tears,___ I could of-fer you a warm em-brace___
I could hold you for a mil-lion years___

1.
to make you feel my love.___
2.
to make you feel my love.___

I know you have-n't made your mind up yet,___ but I would nev-er do___ you wrong.___
The storms are rag-ing on the roll-ing sea,___ and on the high-way of re-gret___

I've known it from the mo-ment that we___ met;___
the winds of change are blow-ing wild and free;___

26

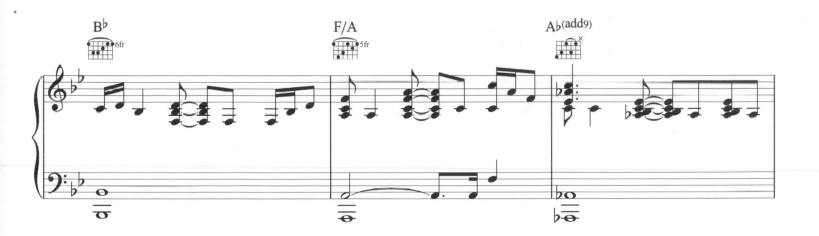

D.S. al Coda

to make you feel my love.

Just The Way You Are

Words & Music by Ari Levine, Bruno Mars, Philip Lawrence,
Peter Hernandez, Khari Cain & Khalil Walton

Her laugh, her laugh, she hates, but I think it's so sex - y.

She's so beau - ti - ful and I tell her ev - 'ry

day. Oh you know, you know, you know I'd nev - er

ask you to change. If per-fect's what you're search-ing for then just stay the same. So

girl, you're a - maz - ing____ just____ the way____ you are...

When I see your face,____

there's not a thing____ that I____ would change____

'cause you're a - maz - ing____ just____

the way you are. And when you smile,

the whole world stops and stares for a while.

'Cause girl, you're a-maz-ing just

the way you are. Yeah.

Pack Up

Words & Music by Tim Woodcock, Matthew Prime,
Felix Powell, Eliza Caird & George Asaf

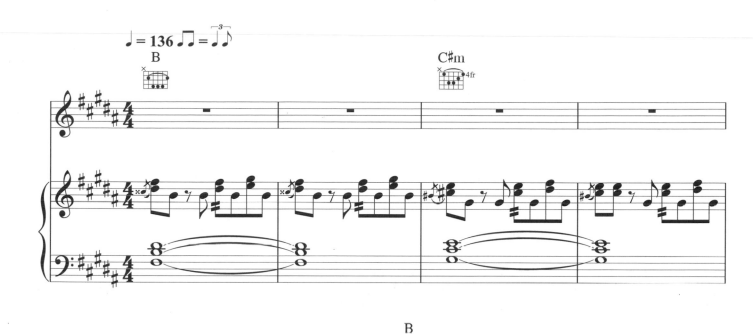

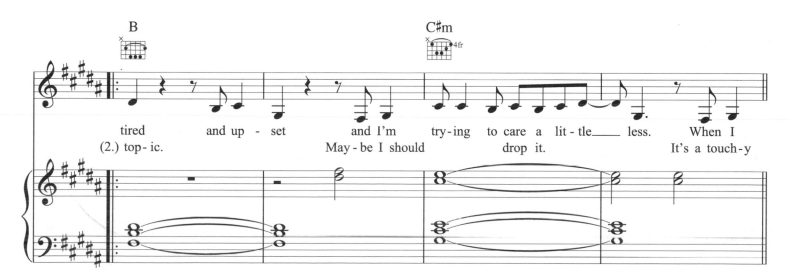

whis - per too loud for me._____

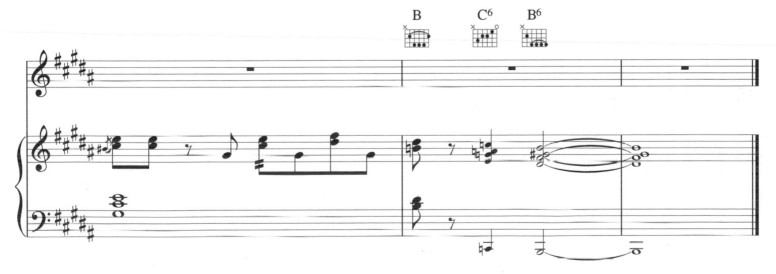

Speechless

Words & Music by Stefani Germanotta

hands up, ba - by you gave up,___ you gave___ up. I___
heart seams, all my bub - ble dreams,___ bub - ble___ dreams. I___

can't be - lieve___ how you looked at me___ with your James Dean glos - sy eyes.___ In your
can't be - lieve___ how you looked at me___ with your John - ny Walk - er eyes.___ He's gon - na

tight jeans with your long hair and your cig - ar - ette stained___ lies.___
get you and aft - er he's through there's gon' be no love left to___ rye.___

___ Could we___ fix___ you if you broke___ and is your punch___
___ And I know that it's com - pli - ca - ted, but I'm a los - er in love. So ba - by, raise a glass to mend all the

She's Always A Woman

Words & Music by Billy Joel

al - ways a wom-an_____ to me.

Oh,_____ she takes care of her-self,_____

she can wait if she_____ wants, she's a-head of her_____

____ time._____

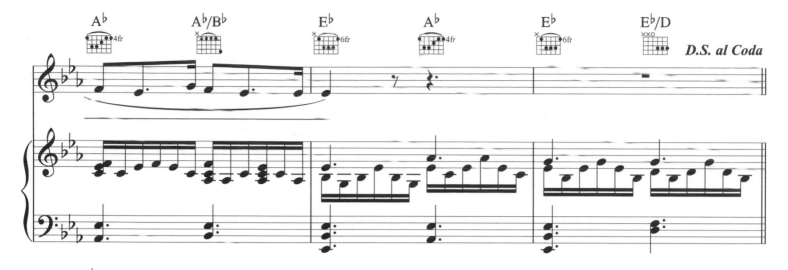

D.S. al Coda

Coda

She is fre-quent-ly kind____ and she's sud-den-ly cruel.____

Well, she can do as she plea - ses, she's no-bod-y's fool.

And she can't be con-vic-ted, she's earned____ her de-gree.__ And the

53

23456789

CD Track Listing

Full performance demonstration tracks...

1. Cry Me Out
(Lott/Hauge/ Thornalley/Campsie)
Universal Music Publishing MGB Limited/Sony/ATV Music Publishing (UK) Limited

2. Empire State Of Mind II
(Keys/Robinson/Carter/Hunte/Keyes/Shuckburgh/Sewell)
EMI Music Publishing Limited/IQ Music Limited/Global Talent Publishing

3. Halo
(Tedder/Knowles/Bogart)
Kobalt Music Publishing Limited/Sony/ATV Music Publishing/EMI Music Publishing Limited

4. Make You Feel My Love
(Dylan) Sony/ATV Music Publishing (UK) Limited

5. Just The Way You Are
(Levine/Mars/Lawrence/Hernandez/Cain/Walton)
Bug Music Ltd/Universal/MCA Music Limited/EMI Music Publishing Limited/
Warner/Chappell Music North America Limited

6. Pack Up
(Woodcock/Prime/Powell/Caird/Asaf)
Francis Day & Hunter Limited/Sony/ATV Music Publishing/
Universal Music Publishing Limited/BMG Rights Management (UK) Limited

7. Speechless
(Germanotta) Sony/ATV Music Publishing (UK) Limited

8. She's Always A Woman
(Joel) EMI Songs Limited

Backing tracks only (without piano)...

9. Cry Me Out

10. Empire State Of Mind II

11. Halo

12. Make You Feel My Love

13. Just The Way You Are

14. Pack Up

15. Speechless

16. She's Always A Woman

To remove your CD from the plastic sleeve,
lift the small lip to break the perforations.
Replace the disc after use for convenient storage.